True
Friendship

This book belongs to

© 2001 Modus Vivendi Publishing Inc.
All rights reserved.

Published by:
Modus Vivendi Publishing Inc.
3859 Laurentian Autoroute
Laval, Quebec
Canada H7L 3H7

Cover and inside page design: Marc Alain
Translation by: Mary Martin

Picture Credits: © SuperStock and Digitalvision

Legal Deposit: 1st Quarter 2001
National Library of Canada

Canadian Cataloguing in Publication Data
Desbois, Hervé
    True friendship
    (Heartfelt Series)
    Translation of: L'amitié
    ISBN: 2-89523-054-4
    1. Friendship. 2. Friendship - Pictorial works.
    I. Title. II. Series
BF575.F66D4713 2001   177'.62   C00-942052-5

Canadä We acknowledge the financial support of the Government
of Canada through the Book Publishing Industry Development
Program (BPIDP) for our publishing activities.

true
Friendship

HERVÉ DESBOIS

MV PUBLISHING

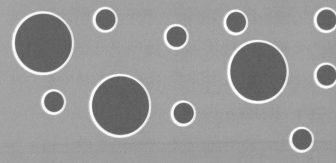

> "Faithful friends are beyond price:
> No amount can balance their worth."

Bible (Old Testament) Sirach 6:15

"Would you like to be my friend?" With these words our search for an alter ego begins at a very early age. A kindred spirit, our confidant, someone who can understand us even in silence, somebody who'll listen to all our secrets without judging us. A friend loves us come what may. A friend accepts us just as she found us. Maybe it's the sister or brother we never had, somebody so much like we are, a mirror reflecting another image of ourself. True friendship isn't interested in changing; it's a blanket that comforts without suffocating.
Friendship can be quiet and attentive, a willing ear and a caring gaze, and, at base, a great source of comfort. Words of friendship are as sweet as honey when we need consolation; they're strong as white-water rapids when it comes to words of encouragement. What a great gift it is to have a friend.

> "A friend is a gift you give yourself."

Robert Louis Stevenson

Friendship

A ruddy drop of manly blood
The surging sea outweighs;
The world uncertain comes and goes,
The lover rooted stays.
I fancied he was fled,
And, after many a year,
Glowed unexhausted kindliness
Like daily sunrise there.
My careful heart was free again-
O friend, my bosom said,
Through thee alone the sky is arched,
Through thee the rose is red,
All things through thee take nobler form
And look beyond the earth,
The mill-round of our fate appears
A sun-path in thy worth.
Me too thy nobleness has taught
To master my despair;
The fountains of my hidden life
Are through thy friendship fair.

Ralph Waldo Emerson

> "No lapse of time or distance of place
> can lessen the friendship of those who are
> truly persuaded of each other's worth."

Unknown

It was 1975. Lost in the middle of the countryside, we were in an out-ot-the-way place whose only citizens were sheep. But that was exactly where my friend and I wanted to be on this vacation. We were intending to reach the Mediterranean by way of footpaths that crisscross the plateaus of Upper Provence. Day after day, we followed the rugged, pebble-strewn paths under the bright sunshine. The magnificence of nature, the beautiful views, the air rich in blossoms and grasses! We travelled without planning where we would stay, so that every day the trip would give us freedom to choose. One thing we knew, though: We wanted to sleep outside as much as possible, to be lulled by the night's symphony, those sounds that unnerved us at first but then gave us deep, peaceful slumber. On our very first day, before we'd even covered fifteen kilometers, I realized I had left behind a bag of food.

"That's bad luck. We'll never make it to the next village," I said, a little crankily.

Christopher made a quick examination of our plight. Even if we were to walk at a good clip, the next village would still be some two days away.

"But we weren't far from a village this afternoon, and it's only 4 o'clock," he said, and before I had a chance to disagree, he was already taking giant strides along the path.

"Okay, but I'm the one who should be going," I yelled after him.

"My legs are longer than yours," were his parting words before he disappeared from sight. True enough, he took about two steps for every three of mine. I resigned myself to unpacking everything for the night, and did it very quickly. Then I decided to spend a moment with one of my favourite vices. "All right. A cigarette will calm me down."

I went through my pockets and came up with a wrinkled blue package that held but one cigarette. Preoccupied by concerns only a smoker can understand, I emptied my knapsack. Imagine my frustration when I discovered I had also left my stash of cigarettes at home. And Christopher a non-smoker. I fumed as my last Gauloise burned down while, distractedly, I made a meal out of the meagre supply we had. I dreaded two long days with no nicotine.

"And to think Christopher went into town."

I wallowed in my frustration for two hours, awaiting Christopher's return. I was in a pretty rotten mood by the time he made it back, all smiles. As he unwrapped the precious food essential to our hike, he talked about the town's beauty. I saw that he was aware of how surly I'd become, even though he didn't mention it. I kept my lip buttoned.

"Oh, yes. I brought this for you too," and he threw me two blue packages, which I recognized right off.

"But I didn't even ask. How did you know?"

"I knew. That's enough!"

"What is a friend? A single soul in two bodies."

Aristotle

Recipe for Friendship

If aphrodisiacs can enhance pasions of lovers all around the world, what are the chances there is a recipe to make friendship grow and strengthen its bonds? As much as I've searched through my books of spells and other reference tools for witches, I couldn't find any incantation or magic potion to enchant a friend out of the blue.

Then I realized all I had to do was to rummage through my own memories to hit on the right recipe, and there's nothing magic about it. It's altogether perfect to create a friendship or to make one stronger: a good meal!

One day a friend of mine hosted one of those rare dinner parties where the laughter blends with the aroma of the food that filled the house. He chose to devote the evening to fondue, although I wouldn't suggest that sort of menu for those with delicate stomachs. For openers, we were treated to a fondue bourguignon—beef and vegetables cooked in red wine. What followed was a fondue Savoyard, to be followed by the finishing touch, chocolate fondue. And you know the evening was long and liberally doused with wine.

(...)

Here is the recipe for fondue Savoyarde, or cheese fondue, just like my grandmother used to make:
For four friends, you'll need:
- 1$^{1}/_{2}$ to 2 pounds of Gruyère cheese
- 3 glasses of dry white wine
- 1 small glass of Kirsch (optional)
- 1 or 2 garlic cloves
- nutmeg, salt, pepper to taste
- bread

Cube the bread and let it dry so that it doesn't fall apart on your fork. Grate or cube the cheese. Ideally, you should use two sorts of Gruyère, like emmenthal (or Swiss) and comté. Rub the garlic on the fondue dish, pour in the wine and warm over medium heat. Once the wine is hot, add the cheese little by little, all the while stirring the mixture with a wooden spoon. Once the fondue reaches the right consistency, you can add a pinch or 2 of nutmeg, the Kirsch, then the salt and pepper to taste. Bring the fondue to the table and keep it warm over the heat source included with the fondue set. Raw sliced vegetables are delicious with fondue, and a nice dry white wine is a perfect choice to top things off.
Remember! Tradition has it that if you lose a piece of bread in the fondue, you must pay up in some way or another. The most popular way is to kiss whoever is sitting at your left. It's up to you to make up your own rules. There'll be lots of laughs if you use your imagination.

"I count myself in nothing else so happy
As in a soul rememb'ring my good friends."

William Shakespeare

"Thus nature has no love for solitude,
and always leans, as it were, on some support;
and the sweetest support is found
in the most intimate friendship."

Cicero

"The friendship that can cease
has never been real."

Saint-Jerome

"I find friendship to be like wine,
raw when new, ripened with age,
the true old man's milk and restorative cordial."

Thomas Jefferson

"Friends have all things in common."

Plato

Are You my Friend?

Written with a pen,
Sealed with a kiss.
If you're my friend please answer this —
Are we friends or are we not?
You told me once but I forgot.
Tell me now and tell me true,
So I can say,
"I'm here for you"
Of all the friends I've ever met,
You're the one I won't forget.
And if I die before you do,
I'll go to Heaven and wait for you.
If you're not there on Judgement Day,
I'll know you went the other way.
I'll give the angels back their wings,
And risk the loss of everything.
Just to prove my friendship true,
I'll go to hell to be with you.

> **"The best mirror is an old friend."**
>
> George Herbert

There was Ségolène, there was Veronica, there was George, and there was me—two close friends and two women we hardly knew going on a week-end adventure. We left on the spur of the moment one beautiful Friday night. We wanted to see the ocean and breathe some fresh air. George and I had been friends since we sat on the benches at nursery school. Ségolène and Veronica, on the other hand, shared a much more recent connection, but youth attracts youth, as though all that was required to cement their friendship was that they were both twenty. They took us up on our invitation without hesitation. Oh, how they laughed when they got into George's old jalopy, a Citroën that was probably older than the hills. Later the smiles turned into something less pleasant when, on the shoulder of the road, the old thing gave up the ghost. Why did the car decide to leave us like that in the middle of the countryside that night? It appears that some questions have no answers. Then, as soon as the racket the engine made gave way to a vast silince, the hellish sound of rain began.

"Great. Now it's raining." Veronica was losing her good mood as quickly as the water from the heavens poured through the roof, which was very quickly indeed.

"Okay, guys, it was really nice of you to invite us to the beach, but what are we going to do now?" Ségolène's feelings were about the same as Veronica's. George began to laugh his best laugh, and all I could do was echo him because the situation was so wacky. Our two guests weren't cheerful a

(...)

all; Ségolène got hysterical, which soured things for good.

George proved himself a prince. "The next town is only two kilometers away. I'll go and get a tow truck."

"Don't even think about it," yelled Veronica. "I'm not staying here. It's deserted and so dark."

"Me neither," said Ségolène, upping the ante.

Then the two women got out of the car and began walking, all the while muttering and cursing. We followed on their heels as fast as we could. The rain suddenly came down twice as hard. Within a few seconds we were soaked to the bone. In half an hour we entered the only café that was still open in the village. Our feet were muddy and our hair rivers of water. Our arrival made a grand impression on the customers, who talked loudly as they played cards. Ségolène rushed to the telephone. George soon found out that the garage wouldn't open again until the morning, if then, depending on the mood of the owner, who was just then losing his shirt. Ségolène, who had just got off the phone, had a determined look in her eyes as she came over to us.

"Sorry, guys, we're taking a cab out of here."

Just like that, the two women went into the night. We heard the sound of the car doors slamming, then the rapidly disappearing sound of the engine. We were alone, without a car, in a desolate village, far from the ocean. George looked at me and started to laugh.

"Ha! When all else fails, there's always the most important thing of all: friendship."

How to Nourish Friendship

Where does friendship grow? Or, rather, how is a friendship born between two people? You'd have to be pretty wise to know the answer to that question, for friendship, following the example of love, can start with a single look, as though a subtle and mysterious energy comes into being with this one contact between two human beings. As well, friendship can grow like things do in nature, taking its time, day by day, patiently but with great strength.

Aristotle wrote that there are three types of friendships, founded on usefulness, joy or virtue. Personally, even though I find friends can indeed be very useful, and that friendship should possess something virtuous, there's no doubting the joy we share when I invite my friends over. There are at least two things that I like to set out for them: fine wine and a lovely dessert.

As far as making wine goes, I'll leave that to the masters. However, here's an all-purpose dessert that you can alter according to your tastes, and those of your guests: a Swiss roll.

(...)

Serves 4 people:
- 3 eggs
- 100 g/6 cups of powdered sugar
- 80 g/3 cups of flour
- 50 g/2 ounces of butter, melted
- pinch of salt
- filling of your choice

Separate the whites from the yolks, then mix the yolks with the sugar to create a whitish paste. Preheat the oven to 200º C/400º F. Salt the egg whites and mix until they form peaks. Gently and quickly add half the flour to the sugar and yolk mix, then half of the egg-white mixture, then the rest of the flour, then the rest of the whites and, finally, the melted butter. Place a sheet of buttered wax paper on a large, rectangular cookie sheet (I use one that is 15^1/2 inches by 10^1/2 inches, or 40 centimeters by 27 centimeters). Pour the batter so it's about 1 centimeter/^{1}/2 inch thick and smooth it out so it's even. Bake for about 10 minutes. Remove from the oven and immediately turn it over onto a clean dish towel. Peel off the wax paper and quickly spread your filling on it (jam, melted chocolate, or whatever you choose). Use extreme care and roll it up. You can pour more of the filling over the roll, use a fruit sauce or serve as is.

"True friendship's laws are by this rule express'd,
Welcome the coming, speed the parting guest."

Alexander Pope

"I no doubt deserve my enemies,
but I don't believe I deserved my friends."

Walt Whitman

"We always thought we'd look back
on our tears and laugh, but we never thought
we'd look back on our laughter and cry."

Unknown

"True friendship is never serene."

Marquise de Sévigné

"Grief can take care of itself, but to get
the full value of joy you must have somebody
to divide it with."

Mark Twain

Sonnet

When to the sessions of sweet silent thought
I summon up remembrance of things past,
I sigh the lack of many a thing I sought,
And with old woes new wail my dear time's waste:
Then can I drown an eye, unused to flow,
For precious friends hid in death's dateless night,
And weep afresh love's long since cancelled woe,
And moan th' expense of many a vanished sight.
Then can I grieve at grievances foregone,
And heavily from woe to woe tell o'er
The sad account of fore-bemoaned moan,
Which I new pay as if not paid before.

But if the while I think on thee, dear friend,
All losses are restored and sorrows end.

William Shakespeare

"A friend in need is a friend indeed"

"I went to pieces." Of course this expression is an exaggeration, but it describes perfectly what happened to me. I was twenty years old and madly in love, sure of myself and my brilliant and promising future; my dreams were everything. The woman I loved and I were on the same path, and nothing could stop us. Nothing except ourselves. Why did things start to go wrong? Is it laziness that keeps us from seeing clearly, that makes us ignore our sixth sense, leaving it to scream in the darkness? One simple letter, a few words scribbled on a sheet of paper—enough to turn the world upside down. The castles we had imagined so solid tumbled like a cheap house of cards. And afterward, there was nothing left. Yet what you think is nothing is, in reality, chaotic, contradictory emotions that drown all reason. When the pain is too great, you need to share it with someone; that's the only way out.

I hadn't seen Francis for months, yet one night I knocked on his door. It was after 11. That familiar round smiling face welcomed me. Francis was going over his notes for a class that had an exam the next morning. I didn't have to say a word. Francis completely understood in a glance, as if my pain had projected itself directly into his thoughts. "All right, tell me."

(...)

What followed was an eruption of jumbled words and mostly confused sentences, all bathed in tears and sobs. I talked all night. He listened attentively to me all night, simply nodding his head from time to time. Then, at first light, Francis invited me to go out for some air. The exam, the university— none of that had any importance for him any more—all that counted was that he had a friend in trouble. While we walked, Francis talked, but not to cheer me up, nor to point out my mistakes, nor even to give me advice...not at all. He knew that anything like that only throws a person ever more deeply into his failure. All he said to me was simply that life is a series of events, happy or sad, that we must face up to as so many trials with only one judge: life itself.

"Sometimes you can do it alone. Other times you need others." Then Francis stopped and looked me right in the eye. "Thank you for having come to me for help. Your trust touches me. I'll always be there."

That day when I left Francis's house, my mind was more at ease. Of course, there were a few more tears and sad moments, and it took some time to digest it all, but just his company gave me the shot in the arm that I needed then.

It's a small world, but a vast planet, and I haven't seen him since. If I were to dedicate this book to somebody, it would be to Francis. Without knowing it, he was one of my greatest friends. Even I didn't realize it until much later, and when I did, I cried.

> **"The better part of one's life consists of friendship."**
>
> Abraham Lincoln

A Rainy Night
in New Orleans

It was a rainy night in New Orleans;
At a bus station in the town,
I watched a young girl weeping
As her baggage was taken down.

It seems she'd lost her ticket
Changing buses in the night.
She begged them not to leave her there
With no sign of help in sight.

The bus driver had a face of stone
And his heart was surely the same.
"Losing your ticket's like losing cash money,"
He said, and left her in the rain.

Then an old Indian man stood up
And blocked the driver's way
And would not let him pass before
He said what he had to say.

"How can you leave that girl out there?
Have you no God to fear?
You know she had a ticket.
You can't just leave her here.

You can't put her out in a city
Where she doesn't have a friend.
You will meet your schedule,
But she might meet her end."

The driver showed no sign
That he'd heard or even cared
About the young girl's problem
Or how her travels fared.

So the old gentleman said,
"For her fare I'll pay.
I'll give her a little money
To help her on her way."

He went and bought the ticket
And helped her to her place
And helped her put her baggage
In the overhead luggage space.

"How can I repay," she said,
"The kindness you've shown tonight?
We're strangers who meet again
A mere 'thank you' doesn't seem right."

He said, "What goes around comes around.
This I've learned with time - -
What you give, you always get back;
What you sow, you reap in kind.

Always be helpful to others
And give what you can spare;
For being kind to strangers,
We help angels unaware."

Unknown

"Take us for example…
Why should we have met? How did it happen?
It can only be that something
in our particular inclinations
made us come closer and closer
across the distance that separated us,
the way two rivers flow together."

Madame Bovary, Flaubert

"My friends are my estate.
Forgive me then the avarice to hoard them.
They tell me those who were poor early
have different views of gold.
I don't know how that is.
God is not so wary as we,
else He would give us no friends,
lest we forget Him."

Emily Dickinson

My Friend,
the Things that do attain

My friend, the things that do attain
The happy life be these, I find;
The riches left, not got with pain;
The fruitful ground, the quiet mind;

The equal friend; no grudge, no strife;
No charge of rule, nor governance;
Without disease the healthy life;
The household continuance;

The mean diet, no dainty fare;
Wisdom joined with simpleness;
The night discharged of all care,
Where wine the wit may not oppress;

The faithful wife, without debate;
Such sleeps as may beguile the night.
Content thyself with thine estate;
Neither wish death, nor fear his might.

Henry Howard

"The happiest moments my heart knows
are those in which it is pouring forth
its affections to a few esteemed characters."

Thomas Jefferson

"Friendship that flows from the heart cannot
be frozen by adversity, as the water that flows
from the spring cannot congeal in winter."

James Fenimore Cooper

"This communicating of a man's self
to his friend works two contrary effects;
for it redoubleth joy, and cutteth griefs in half."

Francis Bacon

"The most I can do for my friend is simply
to be his friend. I have no wealth to bestow
on him. If he knows that I am happy
in loving him, he will want no other reward.
Is not friendship divine in this?"

Henry David Thoreau

"Without friends no one would choose to live,
though he had all other goods."

Aristotle